I0192810

CORPSE AND FLEA

Poems & Pictures
By
Ron Brunk

Copyright © 2014 by Ron Brunk

All rights reserved. All words and drawings contained herein were created by Ron Brunk This book or any portion thereof may not be reproduced or used in any manner whatsoever without the express written permission of the publisher or author except for the use of brief quotations in a book review.

ISBN-13: 978-0692202371 (Alexia Publishing)

ISBN-10: 0692202374

Printed in the United States of America

Alexia Publishing
PO Box 120942
Nashville, TN 37212
www.AlexiaPublishing.com

www.RonBrunk.com
ronbrunk@yahoo.com

Contents

ILLUSTRATIONS

CORPSE AND FLEA

Poems & Pictures
By
Ron Brunk

BREAKING RANK

I once walked in step
With cultural expectations,
Bending ever to the forms
And dictates imposed
By societal norms
That came in winged swarms
Of wasp-shaped shackles,
Armed full with stingers
And howling like jackals.

Then I broke rank
And set out alone.

Some may condemn
While others condone,
But the path that I follow
Is always my own.

◊◊ DIAMONDS ◊◊

Angels cannot comprehend
What mortal man can do,
When he comes to the end of his rope,
Battered black and blue.
Life like a dripping faucet,
Love like a wounded bird;
All his bright tomorrows
Captured in one word.
He knows it's all or nothing,
Clutching wind and dirt;
Finding bits of beauty
Hidden among the hurt.
Diamonds in his spirit
Glimmer in the dark;
Bounding unencumbered
In the kingdom of his heart.

AGING GRACEFULLY IS A DYING ART

I'm starting to show my age;
It shouldn't be a disgrace.
These wrinkles are Experience
Crawling across my face.
Nips, tucks and surgeries;
Botox, pills and creams;
We chase the fountain of youth,
No matter how crazy it seems.
The old man I see in the mirror
Still thinks that he's a kid;
He has this misconception
He can do the things he did.
He's full of these foolish notions,
But I must admire his grit;
He won't take No for an answer,
And he doesn't know when to quit.
Growing old is a tough nut,
And I wish I could say I've cracked it.
Though I'm starting to show my age,
I hope I never act it.

THIS PEACE, I THINK

This peace, I think, would last forever;
This sitting, this watching of the wind;
This unawareness of distraction,
It could go on and on;

If the world were not quite so clever,
And the trees would quit their grin;
Up and down the highway in constant action,
While the autos stand in the lawn.

MAN AND PLOW

A man, as far as usefulness,
Is often like a plow;
His broken ground is equal to
The pushing he'll allow.

MARTIANS

I've wondered long for many hours
Just where Martians plant their flowers,
If there are any (Martians, that is).

It seems to me with dirt *that* red,
Every flower would soon be dead
From jealously (no one likes to be outdone).

I believe if I lived there
And had no flowers anywhere,
And saw my neighbor planet's lush
Flower garden, I would blush.
For Mars has only underbrush
Compared to Earth. I would rush
To join the human race.
Wouldn't you?

It doesn't take a scientist
To prove that Martians don't exist.

CATATONIC

When the poor little bird
Slammed into the window,
Pain seemed a certainty
And death a distinct possibility.
I wept for the tiny creature
As it lay motionless in the dirt.
Clouds shifted in the sky,
A butterfly flitted by,
And just as I
Began to move,
The bird shuddered
And fluttered its wings.
Joy leapt in my heart
As the bird took flight;
I was happy as a child
On Christmas Eve night,
Until it turned and flew
With every bit of its might
Back against the window,
Hard against the glass,
As if possessed by some
Inexplicable urgency to regain
The glass-induced pain
That comes from beating one's head
Against the wall,
Or the catatonic bliss
That follows our rage
When we cast ourselves headlong
Against the bars of our cage.

THE MYSTERY OF IT ALL

Life is what you make it,
And fate is what you do;
It depends on your perspective,
And how *you* look at *you*.

Some are born with a silver spoon,
While others get the fork;
Everyone comes into the world
At the mercy of the stork.

In the window of opportunity
You may only get one pane;
And even where the sky's the limit,
You might only get the rain.

No one here has yet uncovered
The mystery of it all;
But if I do
I promise you,
You'll be the first person I call.

LET GO

There's a supernova
Turning over
Every unturned stone
Inside my head.
There's a gravity
Sucking me
Back down into
The things you said.
There's a galaxy
Spinning free
Inside of me,
And it's telling me
It's time to let go.

I don't believe
How you wind and weave
From revelation
To Adam and Eve.
I must confess
I'm a bloody mess
In my nakedness,
But I digress.
Linear reasoning
Holds no sway
On my circular state
Of mind today.
It's time to let go.

I hear tiny voices
Of distant choices
I once made

Like lemonade
Under the bright sun
Of a cloudless day
When the consequences
Seemed so far away.
What we reap is what we sow,
And we only gain by letting go.
It's time to let go.

CONSTELLATION LESSON ☼☼☼☼☼☼☼☼

Those Seven Sisters live far apart
But to the eye seem very near.
They smile and wink at one another
And at me, too, standing here.

They never fuss or raise their voice;
As far, that is, as we can tell.
No one here that I have known
Could get along quite that well.

They're close enough to care and speak,
But never too close to knock
Another off from where she is
With an elbow or a rock.

Their stellar heat by frigid space
Is given room to burn.
Perhaps we need to face the fact
That there's something there to learn.

THE MOON)

I am like the moon;
I follow the spell of a lunar tune;
Wandering through the night
With each progressive sliver.
The essence of my light
Generates a shiver.
I am, at times, eclipsed;
But sometimes the eclipser.

CORPSE AND FLEA

Discovering the man's body to be an impediment in
his excursion,
The flea decided it best
To jump upon the chest
Of the lifeless frame
And continue same
Upon his quest.
But once upon it, he found himself curious;
This creature called man lived a life luxurious.
So realizing his chance,
He began a tour,
Fearing not the least
For this man was no more.
(Fleas know about things like bodies on floors.)

He leaped to the cheek and took a bite,
And enjoyed the view with great delight;
Then spotted the man's hair
And quickly dove there,
And rummaged wildly until fully satisfied.
He was so happy this man had died!

But as time is precious in the life of a flea,
He reigned himself in from this festivity,
Then bounced precariously along thigh and shin,
Sauntered right round and back up again.
Suddenly, while crossing the chest toward home,
A voice arose from beneath the breastbone
(For everyone knows that's where the soul dwells);
The voice of a soul still between heaven and hell,
And it queried the flea as to his purpose there.

14

To which the flea replied, "That's my affair."
Then he fired back quickly a question of his own:
"Why do you, soul, still here remain?"

"I cannot depart until the body has been claimed."

"But I have found you," said the flea. "Have I not?"

"Yes, but you are only a flea, a meaningless dot.
I must be found by a loved one –
A father, sister, cousin or aunt –
By something more than a spot."

Taken aback by such hostile disposition,
The flea set about defending his position.
He challenged the man's soul:
"Who are you to assess my worth?
You are only an intangible within a corpse.
You no longer exist, you have no say;
Whereas I am living – I can go on my way."

Not the least bit unnerved
(For the spirits of men are a brave lot),
The soul of this man
Voiced his thoughts
Clearly and arrogantly
(For the thoughts of men are tremendously proud).
"Flea," said the spirit, "you are a perpetual infant,
Mindless and without purpose.
You cannot reason, feel, nor achieve.
Why, you don't even know why you breathe.
But I, I am the soul of a man,
And man is the greatest of all creatures!

He is adaptable, logical, and wise;
Man can experience emotional ties.
He juggles with ease his past and his fate
With theories and weapons both small and great;
From microchip calculations
To neurotransmitter manipulations,
Mathematics, linguistics, astronomy,
Botany, physics, and philosophy;
Horticulture, chemistry, biology,
Criminology, cosmetology, and geology;
Meteorology, psychology, sociology,
Every conceivable cutting-edge technology,
And, *of course*, you must be aware of entomology.
With all of these –ologies impressive indeed,
We're bigger and better with always more speed!
Man is Lord and Master of the earth,
Destined to rule from the day of his birth,
As decreed by Almighty God himself!
But you, flea, what have you won?
What do you have to show for what you've done?"

The flea laughed as he spat upon the cold, hard flesh
And sped away.

A MAN'S PREROGATIVE

I know I should be working, doing
Something more than sitting, chewing
On this blade of grass, I feel.
But nothing in me says I will.

LOVE AND HARSH REALITY

Roses are red,
Violets are blue;
I'm falling in love,
But not with you.

BEDTIME PRAYER

Now I lay me down to sleep;
I pray the Lord my soul to keep.
If I should die before I wake,
Someone please resuscitate.

A SUMMER RAIN

I sat to watch a summer rain;
It paid no mind to me.
But something in its falling free
Paralleled my inner pain.

I could not help but sympathize
With what it tried to do.
While casting down itself it knew
The Earth was twice its size.

It spent itself and with a sigh,
Stopped raining all at once,
As if to proclaim innocence
Of all I saw it try.

But tiny rills on tops of hills,
And sediment down below,
Were evidence enough to show
The fight was an act of Will.

I sat to watch a summer rain
Against Earth a battle wage;
Who would believe such outward rage
Could so ease my inner pain?

IMPORTANT MATTERS

His eyes dance about,
Darting here, then there;
Nothing wrong anywhere –
But so many possibilities!

He sees imaginary baskets
That balls slip through as the clock winds down;
Nothing but net with a swishing sound.

He bends at the waist and reads the signs,
Winds up tightly and hurls it straight
To catcher crouching behind the plate.

Last comes a dare,
From an invisible foe;
Left hooks fly
And he lays him low.

Then he heads for home;
He's got things to do.
Boys have important matters
They must attend to.

THE THINGS WE FEAR

One sand hornet by a stump
Buzzes by and makes us jump
Though there's no stinger in his rump.

And even more extraordinaire
Is when we face an angry bear
Who made our garbage his affair.

Or when we hear a late-night knocking
As if a burglar softly stalking
Found a door that had no locking.

Or when we think of bombs so great
That man will soon annihilate
Himself (as if that were his fate).

We act as though the world were ours,
As if by some internal powers,
We determine days and hours.

I think it is we mostly fear
(From coast to coast and year to year)
That we determine nothing here.

BELOW THE SURFACE

I take a drink of water,
But rarely give a thought
To how I came to hold each glass
Of water that I've got.
I reach and turn the faucet
And open up the spout,
As if I had an inkling
Of what water's all about.
I know the water flows
When I turn the faucet round,
But I fail to see the forces
There at work beneath the ground.
Sometimes hot, sometimes cold,
It runs a lot like me,
Through many miles of hidden lines
That others rarely see.
I've never fully understood
The working of it all;
With so much below the surface,
Or well hidden behind a wall.

A GRAVE VISIT

We walked a while
To find the spot
Where he was laid
To place a pot
Of flowers bright
Upon the grave
(With inward fear
But outward, brave).

Our little girl
No more than two,
Pulled up some grass
And lost her shoe.
He did not live
To see her born;
They missed by days –
She could not mourn.
Our memory
Could not hers be;
Blood was *their* tie,
Not memory.

the afterthought:

A memory
Is like a stew
That when re-heated
Tastes like new.
And spooning out
You seek the part

That tastes the best
And warms your heart.
So there beside
That grave of earth,
We stirred our stew
And spooned for mirth.

Brunk

THE CHOICE WAS OURS

Like master in the Master Race,
With right to save or to erase,
We cleared our land as if it were ours…
Though it wasn't.

A tree long fallen and rotted some,
Was lifted leaving bits and crumbs,
And there beneath we spied a bug, but…
We couldn't name it.

It was huge, black and very ugly,
We looked and thought and then quite smugly
Began to stomp, and he to hide, but…
Did we get him?

Dead or hid – we left off there
For the wood that we still had to bear.
If, indeed, he could live through that, well…
Then, he can live.

SORROWS OF THE LAWN

"This land belongs to us!"
And so we make a fuss;
It's a never-ending battle with the weeds.
"This piece of ground is ours!"
So we spend the toilsome hours
With hoe and shovel, rake and seeds.

We fertilize and spray
To keep the pests away;
It's an American middle class disease.
Our lawn must be pristine,
Far and away more green
Than our neighbors have ever seen.

One small, loft apartment, if you please.

OFF COURSE

My self-respect took such a beating;
I bloodied my own nose
With the things that I chose
To believe.

But a lie will serve as your teacher;
In this lip-service world,
That serpent is curled
Up in me.

But the power of Time has no rival;
It wounds as it heals,
And gives as it steals
From your life.

But your life can change in an instant;
Like the wind when it blows
And suddenly throws
You off course.

OPPORTUNISTIC POET

There is no other beauty
That draws the pen to page,
Like that within a sunrise;
It humbles every age,
From youth to hardened sage.

Written of in words and rhyme,
From every angle done;
But I am not discouraged –
No one's written of this one.

OF VERBS AND TENSE

I'm growing up,
I'm growing down,
And all the while
The earth goes round.
A little time
And I will be
A little spot
Of dirt, you see.
The secret here
Is to take hold,
And not let go
Until you're told;
Or better yet,
Until you're forced;
Carpe diem
Until divorced
From this living
That we call Life,
Then thrust upon
Your earthen wife.
But bear in mind
As you go down,
That still the earth
Goes round and round.
Your death makes not
One dif-fer-ence;
You're simply past
Not present tense.

THE BIG GONG

I'm not convinced of evolution,
And if I ran the institution,
I would decree that common sense
Be brought to bear in my defense.
For if we're on an upward track,
Evolving outward from the black,
Improving on the things we lack,
Then why no wings upon my back?
If evolution were so sound,
We wouldn't be forever bound
To lumber always on the ground;
We'd sprout some wings and fly around!
For aerial trumps terrestrial
As birth is better than burial.

☽ NIGHTFALL

I like the day
With my hair thrown back in the sun;
I am not opposed
To any daytime fun.
But I also like the night,
For in it lies the sight
Of things that are not seen in light,
Things that only darkness brings.
Trees become silhouettes
Against a fading sky.
The moon becomes mighty;
I do not ask him why.
The land turns quiet
And voices carry far,
Even to my front porch
And maybe to a star.

We do not know all
There is to know about the night,
But a man must learn this lesson:
There is no other falling
That brings so loud a silence,
And makes such great impression.

PLANET YOU

Orbits come and orbits go,
But you're the only planet I know.
The golden orb is breaking through;
Copernicus revolving you.

Touch down on your surface, see
The many sights awaiting me.
You take me down, you eat me up,
Like barley, hops and buttercup.

Incessantly through your atmosphere,
Absolutely crystal clear;
I strike your surface helplessly,
I'm caught in zero gravity.

Out of chaos, into clear;
You're universal center, dear.
Solar system crashing down;
Black hole spinning on the ground.

Everything we say, everything we do
Revolves around the planet I call YOU.
Everywhere we go, everything we do,
The universe revolves around planet YOU.

THAT DAY

Once we sat in a dingy booth
Eating fresh, hot pizza
At Jack & Joe's hospitable restaurant,
On the muddy banks
Of the oil-slicked Ohio River.
Jack and Joe were gambling bums,
Horse-track hooligans,
Crooked, drug-dealing thieves.
Or so we were told.
But their flashing pinball machine,
Cheap, cheesy pizza,
And thrilling tales
Put them much higher
In our young eyes.
And all the while,
We lived and laughed on
As Graham Nash's "Chicago"
Spun round inside the jukebox,
Meaning nothing.
Return that day to me, dear God,
Return that day to me.

SHOES

Sunday mornings in Westfield
Were light on traffic and noise,
Heavy on eggs, biscuits, gravy, and church.
It was a two-step program
That most of the residents observed religiously –
Food for the belly, food for the soul –
Every Lord's Day morning.
But on this particular Sunday,
Jason Cullen didn't come down to breakfast.

His mother called him once, then again,
And finally once more,
This time with that exasperated voice
That mothers use when their patience is thinning.

Jason heard his mother all three times,
But didn't respond because something,
Something was bothering him.
He had an awful lot on his mind these days;
There was pressure to make important decisions
And to make them soon.
He was dealing with his upcoming graduation,
Peer pressures, parents, hormones, girls,
College choices, sports, job opportunities,
And a thousand other things all at once.
Who was he? Where was he headed?
What should he do with his life?
Jason couldn't decide the answers
To any of these questions;
So now he sat on the edge of his bed,

Unable to decide which shoe to put on first.
Jason never was good with decisions.

Downstairs, breakfast was getting cold
And Jason's mother was becoming perturbed.
"Jenny, go up and see what your brother's doing."

Jenny, three years younger than Jason,
Was always anxious to be involved
In any potential fireworks.
She sprinted up the stairs
And banged on Jason's door.
"Mom wants to know what's taking you so long!"

After a pause, Jason replied,
"I can't decide which shoe to put on first."

"Huh? What are you *talking* about?"

Jason felt like everyone was on his back,
And the irritation was clear in his voice.
"The right one or the left one, stupid.
I can't decide which one to put on first.
Did I stutter or something?"

Jenny rolled her eyes at the closed door,
Then raced back down to the kitchen, shouting,
"Mom, you won't believe it!
He says he can't decide which shoe to put on first."

Mrs. Cullen stared at her husband incredulously.
"Did you hear that?
He can't decide which shoe to put on first.

What is *that* supposed to mean?"
She turned back to Jenny,
"What does he mean? That he can't choose
Between his boots or his sneakers or what?"

"Nope, not that.
He doesn't know whether to put
His right shoe on first or his left one."
Jenny relished these rare occasions
When Jason did something troublesome.
It provided an entertaining diversion
From her otherwise humdrum, daily routine.

Mrs. Cullen stood up and looked at Mr. Cullen
Who was still eating his eggs.
He was trying not to get involved,
But she rebuked him, hands on hips,
With a piercing look and a long, drawn-out,
"Well?"

"What do you want me to do about it?" he asked.

"Go talk to him. You're his father."

He knew there was no use arguing,
So he calmly put down his napkin
And took one more drink of coffee.
Then he pushed his chair back from the table
And headed upstairs to see Jason.
"What's the matter, boy?"

Jason looked straight in his dad's eyes
And said quite matter-of-factly,

"I can't decide whether
To put my left shoe on first
Or my right one on first."

His father sighed,
Ran his left hand over his graying crew cut,
And sat down slowly on the edge of the bed.
Mr. Cullen was a deliberate man of few words
Who rarely spoke without plenty of forethought.
He simply believed that the shortest distance
between two points was a straight line,
And that a man was better off
To focus on the tasks at hand
And keep his words to a minimum.

He looked thoughtfully around his son's room
At the trophies, fishing poles, BB guns,
And calendar of bikini-clad women,
While the silence settled
Like a good rain on a cornfield.
Mr. Cullen knew, as everyone in town did,
That Jason was a fine boy.
Sure, he sometimes had trouble making decisions,
But he was smart, with plenty of potential.
Jason managed to keep his GPA up
While starring on the high school football team –
and he once made 22 solo tackles in a single game!
Coach said the kid had a pretty good shot
At playing college ball.
And last year, he even took
Leigh Brandstetter to the prom,
And everyone knew Leigh
Was one of the prettiest girls in school.

Mr. Cullen sure was proud of his boy,
And he supposed Jason knew
Just how much he loved him.

The old man's hands were leathery and gnarled
from years of farm work,
But they could be tender and loving
When the situation called for it.
Now was one of those times.
Mr. Cullen placed his right hand
On Jason's shoulder
And studied his face for a moment.
"Son, whoever said a man
Had to wear shoes anyway?
Ain't never seen that in the Bible, have you?"

Jason smiled. "No, dad. Don't guess I have."

Jason came down to breakfast
And went to church
Barefoot.

SIMPLY SO

In riddles we speak often,
Flowing over with enigmas,
Metaphors, and analogies
On assets and stigmas.

Still yet, perhaps, certainly
The time has wandered in
For concise registering
Of my mind and path within.

Surely now, of the earth I speak
In tones redolent of Oneness;
Man and all his manly things
Persuade me leaving sonless.

For none the wiser
Would be he who cried
Time on time for things
Now so simplified.

I would leave, yes,
And will, no doubt,
Join all those I've never known
But have been so long without.

THE NOISE

Everywhere around the globe
Enemies clash in battle;
The guns of war exploding,
And men slaughtered like cattle.

Perched upon a red rock height,
A pack of coyotes cries.
Their melancholy cuts the night,
Echoes long before it dies.

Somewhere far along some coast
The sea churns white against
The unyielding shore, its host,
In a battle never quenched.

In a lonely kitchen's gloom
Woman vents on dishes;
Pots and pans sound a tune
To drown unanswered wishes.

The earth takes a valiant stand
As rolling thunder roars,
Pushing hard against the land
From mountains down to shores.

But I slept soundly in my bed,
Despite the world's cacophony;
Until a slight noise overhead
Filtered down and woke me.

Only the faintest sound,
A small rodent, I presumed;
With something it had found
Or recently exhumed.

And when I heard it, I rose up to see;
Aroused because this noise concerned *me*.

WIND AND RAIN

Summer heat is fine, no doubt,
In summertime or days of drought;
But only short and time about
With wind and rain coming out
In turbulent waterspout.
And we sit by window looking out
As elements are blown about
By random winds that seem to flout
Us peering from our station out.
And the rain raps our window loud,
Falling fast from angry cloud,
As if to give a warning sound,
And show us things we've not yet found.

COUNTING RINGS

There is a tree somewhere unfound
That stands without the slightest sound,
And makes no move in haste or fear
Of shining axe head swinging near,
But slowly inches up from ground.

Reaching skyward, I do not know
What it seeks or where it may go,
But lovely are the limbs that strain
Against the pelting snow and rain,
And wind that will not quit its blow.

Year by year yields ring upon ring,
Yet comes an end to everything.
A hundred years of living, growing,
Wiped away in one quick going.
Year by year and ring upon ring;
Now someone buys a wooden thing.

CROW'S FEAT
with a nod & wink to Mr. Robert Frost

The way a crow did buffet me
About a freshly chop-ped tree
Was more than I could face or bear
And so I left off cutting there.

MAGIC WORDS

These soliloquies of silence
That you and I exchange
Burn our well-worn bridges,
And the familiar becomes strange.

I'm inside your skin
And you're inside my brain;
What were once our common threads
Have now become our pain.

The ceiling fan ignores me,
As it spins there undisturbed;
And the TV just goes on as if
I'd never said a word.

Who it is that hears me now,
I guess I'll never know;
Could it be this fragile need
Is everywhere I go?

I wish there were some magic words
That I could say to you;
Magic words
To make this true love
Come true.

A CHANGE OF MIND

Like dew on the dust,
Or smoke on the wind,
One or the other
Must come to an end;
Or both, to allow
The New to begin.
There's a time for yellows
And browns, so serene;
But nothing quite
Compares with green.
"I once thought leaves
To be prettiest red,
But I've changed my mind,"
He, smiling, said.

THE MISSING STAR ˣ

Dotting spots like restless thoughts
Unwinding on a page
Of purest ink black.
They tell us that some,
The more powerful ones,
Have the power of a million of our suns.
We scan and chart them,
Adore and heart them,
Try to outsmart them,
Whether Big Bang or God
It was to start them.
They have our undying attention.
While men die daily on
In numbers clicking steadily upward,
Yet, with barely an eyebrow raised.
But what an uproar there would be
Were we to gaze on high,
Finding even one single star
Missing from the sky.

TWO SHIPS NOT PASSING

Wise by terms unknown to her,
But somehow still sadder, yet;
With guilt that comes from insight,
A delusion born of debt;
Opinion based on circumstance,
Subjective in the short-term,
Like baseless faith or hopeless hope
Standing ever more so firm.

Remain, I will, and so resist,
For there will be the challenge;
Though she may find this rudely cruel
And somewhat out of balance;
If she should return at last
To the terms from which she came;
Forsaking me, thereby, though
She never once knew my name.

WE MUST PARTICIPATE

We find ourselves a quiet place,
A harbor from the din
Of chatter and of busy-ness
And of forces pointed in .

We find ourselves some solitude
Where nothing looms above,
And cradle our so weary head
And determine not to move.

We find ourselves a shady tree
And an acorn right for cracking;
And there upon an earthen bed
We flush the beast we're tracking.

But still there is no kill nor skin,
In spite of all desire.
For you cannot stand on the edge of Time,
Or freeze in the midst of fire.

SELF-PITY

Have you ever seen a cat
In a tussle with its tail?
Or a slowly sulking turtle
Disenchanted with its shell?
It's an old familiar problem,
One I'm feeling all too well:
The grass is always greener
On a lot that's not for sale.

STEP INSIDE

If you could step inside a picture painting
And live the life contained within,
Where passersby seen a finished work,
You would see it just begin.

RELAX

The light of shadows crosses the floor;
Darkness waits beyond your door;
It's only the Future that's there in store;
Relax, there's nothing more.

IF OUR LOVE WAS EGGS

If our love was eggs,
We'd be sunny side up;
With bacon and toast on the side
And hot coffee in a cup.

If our love was eggs,
We'd be over-easy,
With gravy in the skillet,
And sausage not too greasy.

If our love was eggs,
We'd make the perfect omelet;
With mushrooms and peppers,
And cheese melted on it.

If our love was eggs,
We'd scramble every day
In the skillet of love,
You and I would sizzle away.

THE SIX-YEAR SILENCE

You would not dare
To ask a bear
Of six years hibernation,
Why he chose
His eyes to close
For such a long duration.

You would not try
To question why
A storm would cease its rage,
To pass you by
And clear the sky
At such a tender age.

And therefore I
Would not deny
Myself the right to stop
My writing hand
And poet stand
Before I've reached the top.

THE CYCLE

Tired upon a quiet night,
With day gone by and out of sight;
Rotation gives a promised light
Early in the morning.

Thankful for the silent night,
A moment given to invite
The warmness of the firelight
And all its frills adorning.

Men before and men again
Will brace themselves against the wind,
Will muscles strain and hope extend
Early in the morning.

Then wait again for brief respite,
For cycle knows no end despite
The men who are erased, and quite
Quickly without warning.

COFFEEHOUSE CLOSING

A tribute to the famous Serendipity Coffeehouse (owned and operated by Fran & Dick Klaus) upon its closing in 1999.

It isn't simply coffee
That this coffeehouse represents;
There is so much more:
The meeting of minds,
Interchange of information,
Swapping of stories,
And intermingling of a singular spirit.

Many a star-crossed love
Has been conceived and nurtured
Over a cup of coffee.

Many a conversation
Has been held together at times,
Ever so tenuously,
By a cup of coffee.

This coffeehouse has been a haven
For the hungry,
For the haunted,
For the hopeful,
For the hapless hobo
In all of us.

But the day inevitably comes
When we stare into the bottom of an empty cup,
When there are no more beans to be ground,

No more caffeine buzz to be found,
And nothing remains but the clinking sound
Of coffee cups being boxed away.

So take one last look around this room,
Smell the hearty aroma,
Savor the flavor.
Wrap both hands around your cup of coffee
And feel the soothing warmth.
Look into the faces
Of the people you've come to know
Over a cup of coffee.

Close your eyes and remember
The moments and the spirits
That have touched your life in this place.
And have one more cup.
Just one more cup.

A MATTER OF HEMISPHERES

It's hard to think of winter now
With so much bursting out in life;
With wood what whittles with a knife,
And boys that pick a girlish wife.

It's hard to think that someone now
Down under sees things wintery;
For hemispheres aren't much to me,
Though weather differs drastically.

It's hard to think of "down below"
As someplace worth the going to.
It conjures scenes of falling through,
Something I don't plan to do.

ACROSS THE AGES

I sit and wonder sometimes
What it will be like to be older;
With a bit of gray to frost the hair,
To produce that certain experienced air
About me where I go;
With a house that's finally paid in full,
And a pullover sweater made of wool
To warm my well-worn frame;
With proper words on tip of tongue,
A bit of wisdom for the young,
And a mountain of memories;
With gifts for every great-grandchild,
A warning for one that's gone too wild,
And a smile that says, *I was there once, myself.*
I only wish it were possible
To take these characteristics
Across the years uncrossable,
And wear them well at seventeen
Twenty-five, thirty-eight or forty-nine.
But there's life that's ripe for living
At this and every age;
And lines that demand our giving
Before we move from stage to stage.
Life is no more than we make it,
No matter what the age.

THE SURE THING

He took the field in full attire,
With hat and glove and eyes of fire.
No man alive had yet been made
Who could match the way he played.
The game began and bit by bit
Each team scored on hit by hit.
The stands were full – a record crowd;
The game was tight – the fans were loud.
He clutched his glove against his chest,
And felt the pounding in his breast.
With bases full and two men out,
The time had come, there was no doubt.
The batter swung and sent the ball
Long and deep toward the wall.
His eyes were fixed, his muscles taut;
There was no ball he hadn't caught.
He thought of all the years he'd spent,
And how his father, not content
To let him play an average game,
Pushed him hard and fanned his flame.
And all that work would pay off now;
He *knew* he'd catch that ball somehow.
He surged with every ounce of strength,
And stretched his body to its length.
He closed his glove and caught the air;
He must have lost it in the glare.
The ball returned to earth instead,
And hit him squarely on the head.
The call was made; there was no doubt:
The runners safe, but he was out.

LOVE

The depths of love I feel in me
Surpass the things I seek or see.
There's nothing more or less within;
No tender touch, no scent on wind;
Though such should all-inclusive be,
None leaves me waiting breathlessly.

I face the dreaded darkness now.
Should I surface? Should I bow?
Such cumbersome uncertainty
Is ever on the path with me;
And yet our love alone, somehow,
Still keeps me living, hoping now.

BIRD

Her eyelids fluttered
Like the wings of a drunken bird;
Flight interrupted
By something fowl and absurd;
As if aviation
Were a foreign concept and word
To one so grounded
By patterns of regret
And solitude unbounded,
Like the wisps of smoke
From an eternal cigarette.

INVENTION

Man's journey on Planet Earth
Is one of endless
Yearning, learning,
Striving and diving
Into the impossible,
Diving into the impossible,
Diving into the impossible
Until
It eventually becomes
Astoundingly
Commonplace.

CONVENTION

In the end
It will not matter
If your poetry
Does or does not rhyme,
Nor if it marches
To its own obscure
Or unmeasured
Beat or time;
And those who say differently
Are perpetrators of a crime
Against the Ages,
Against humanity,
And everything sublime.

POSSIBILITIES

The world is wide open to you,
And the sky is bright and sunny;
There is nothing you cannot do,
If you have money.

AND SHE

The room was bare
Almost everywhere,
And she had dreadlocks
In her hair.
The setting sun
Was the only one
Going down
Like the kingdom come.
The TV channel
Featured Mickey Mantle
A little more
Than she could handle;
And the web was spun
Like a loaded gun,
And she shot me down
Just to have some fun.

Too much clutter
Made her stutter;
She failed to keep
Her bread and butter
On the night stand
At her right hand
With an open bottle
Of KY jam.
And she slipped off her slip
And took a trip
With a Quaalude melting
On her lip;
And she pictured Reagan
Like a master pagan,

And feared the flesh
Like a virgin vegan.

She bellied up to me
Like a fine beauty;
I couldn't help but wonder
What she'd do to me.
In another life
She may have
Been my wife,
Or perhaps just the cause
Of some bitter strife.

And she talks to me
When I'm sleeping in my bed;
And she takes me
Around the world somewhere in my head.

IT SEEMS WE'RE AT OUR BEST
WHEN WE COMPLAIN

When it rains, we wish it would stop,
And when it's dry, we say we need the rain.
It seems we're at our best when we complain.

Fahrenheit or centigrade degrees –
It makes no difference when the heat is mean,
Or the cold too cold, or too in-between.

Did you hear the way he spoke to me?!
His words were not the wisest choice,
But worse than that was the tone of voice.

This shirt and pants looked so fine before,
But one or the other has, no doubt, faded,
Or stretched or shrunk or become outdated.

Goldilocks syndrome now abounding –
Life is either too hectic or too plain.
It seems we're at our best when we complain.

SNOW VIGIL

I looked out my window
To watch the wind blow
An infinite number of flakes of snow.

It was the type of night
When the world turns white
As if it were shocked to see the snow.

I thought of my son
And what he might become;
I strained to spot his footprints in the snow.

My daughters were sleeping,
So silently keeping
Themselves from the mounting snow.

My sleep eluded me,
But the night included me
In its lonely vigil over the snow.

THE WALL

A twist of fancy, a turn of events,
A change of heart for self-defense;
Two pair of eyes but neither see
The wall we've built so silently.

One half the moon and two faint stars
Smiling out from mason jars;
A wall of clouds across the sky
Now separating you and I.

A shade of blue I've never seen,
Some type of melancholy sheen,
Mostly sorrow, part serene,
Tainting what we say or mean,
Helps build the wall we've never seen.

ROSCOE

When I was a young boy, my best friend,
My only true and faithful friend,
Was my dog, Roscoe.
Roscoe was a friendly, happy, little brown mutt.
And he was the only one who understood me.

There were times in my youth
When my parents would force me
To sit down at the dinner table,
To dine with them,
As if dining could somehow forge a bond
Between ME and THEM,
As if joint food consumption could,
Through some mystical power,
Erase their putrid guilt
And stall my train of grief
Upon the very tracks of my soul.

On one such day, I sat silently with them;
Staring, suffering, stagnating
In contemptuous contemplation;
Stirring my gravy with my spoon,
Seeing dark things in the gravy,
Grisly things,
And bits of hair.
Dog hair.

Roscoe was gone.
But delicious.

BALLAD OF TED MILLS

Pitter patter go the rains from the skies;
Buzz buzz go the flies round his eyes;
Why is it so hard to recognize
That life is only death in disguise?

Streets and hearts are made of stone,
Bones scrape thin against skin;
The world is hard as frozen mud,
And the good old days have never been.

Nothing means nothing, and it never did;
With booze and blood poured on the kid.
It all will fall when it's time has come,
And he will die by the setting sun.

BLAMING THE SUNSHINE

I feel like I'm pressed up against the wall,
Or about to go over the waterfall
In a barrel full of monkeys,
All screaming in my brain.
All you've ever done
Is claim that I was the one
That caused your pain.
That's like blaming the sunshine
For bringing on the rain.

I have moved my last mountain;
I don't have to prove a thing,
Because I have drunk deep from that fountain
Where the angels dip their wings.
The lonely sinner sings
A dirge to ease his pain;
Forever blaming the sunshine
For bringing on the rain.

Kings and angels may fall from grace,
And tears will stain your sweet face;
Your world may crumble
And all your plans could fail;
And they might crucify you
With a hammer and a nail
On a cross of shame;
Still, you're blaming the sunshine
For bringing on the rain.

GRAND DESIGN

I do not like it when the lights go out
And you rearrange my furniture;
Casting doubt on my preconceived notions
With thoughts so lividly impure.
We are not so different, you and I;
Good and evil on one thin dime.
Life eats life to ward off death;
We're victims of the Grand Design.
We stand brazenly on the precipice,
Waving weapons we've employed;
But will waver in the emptiness
Of things we cannot avoid.
We weave and wind our lives like needlepoint,
Yet stop and turn quickly on a pin;
We labor hard to make our point,
Then toss it into the wind.
It's not enough for you to feel my pain;
I'd rather that you take it away;
Years of self-indulgent behavior
Can't be shaken in a day.
It's almost impossible to believe
This random chaos is self-induced;
Rip up the carpet, tear down the walls,
Meet the demon you have loosed.

FORFEIT

I breathe and eat
And cry and walk;
I often stare
And rarely talk.
But I'm always here,
Holding the place
Assigned to me
To compete in the race;
Searching for purpose
In a purposeless place.

But such as I am,
I never will be
Something which is
So loathsome to me;
I cannot compete
In this mockery.

I don't want the Cup
Or even the spoils;
And I'm not such a fool
To enjoy the toils.

The race is too crowded,
Too poorly run,
Cruel and unruly –
These things I shun.

Where Millay once struggled
And clung hard to Life,
I'll welcome Death
In any size slice;
I'll welcome Death,
Not once, but twice.

A PIECE OF NOTHING

See the man, see the boy
Beat his head against the wall;
Clench his fist toward the sky,
Take the bait and the fall.

See the man, see the boy
Close his eyes against the pain;
Clutching to a childhood toy,
Repeats some sad refrain.

Till the ground, turn the soil;
Sixty years of sweat and toil,
All for a piece of nothing.

THE POWER OF DREAMS

I dreamed I was an orange on an apple tree;
No matter how I tried, I could not fit in.
They say that dreams are just fantasy,
But I woke with the smell of citrus on my skin.

A POET'S RIGHTS

If I should frown or seem annoyed,
then that's the best time to avoid
                                        me.
If on the other hand you find
you seem to think I've lost my mind,
                                        be
very careful how you talk
or I may make a fearsome squawk.
                                        See
how I take my own sweet time?
And nothing says I have to rhyme
                            every line, does it?

IDIOTS

I see you drag your feet,
Plodding the evolutionary trail;
Spouting lovely platitudes
While stoking the fires of hell.

You're a bloody, two-faced devil;
Beating on the slave;
You're shallow in the deep end,
A burden to the grave.

IQ is the barometer
That falls when you walk in;
Negative the millibars,
Vacuous in your grin.

It's not so much your ignorance;
Not even just your greed;
It's more that you're an idiot,
Spreading idiot seed.

IN THE AFTERMATH OF WESTERN CIVILIZATION

Too many years spent in the haze
Of those sitcom prosperity days;
Editorial intrusion in my head,
I think I hear what you thought you said.

Man does not live by bread alone,
Plastic cards or Styrofoam;
We trade our faith for vanity;
It's madness wrapped in insanity.

Seems ironic with BHT
Corrupting flesh invisibly;
But that's what you get when you clone
Propaganda, lies and silicone.

I get so tired of narrow-minded people
Who hide away behind a great steeple;
They strain at a gnat and swallow a camel;
Truth is more than they can handle.

Where has the restless troubadour gone?
Superficial lines are drawn;
We're tangled up in the world-wide web;
People scream but nothing's said.

Courage is the thing you find
When you're scared to death and almost blind;
Fear isn't all it's cracked up to be;
Perception is your reality.

Makes no difference where you are,
The black hole sucks the shining star;
It's all so grand, but nothing stays;
Every moment a thousand ways.

We only pass this way one time;
Why not lay it all on the line?
You can love or you can hate;
But please just don't procrastinate.

DRIVING FORCE

We reach, we strive, we break our backs;
We swing on branch until it cracks;
We strike the pose but can't relax.

Not content to let things be
In realm of possibility,
We strain for what we cannot see.

Deep within the heart of man
There is a voice that says, "I can."
And the Driving Force constructs a plan.

The power of this Driving Force
Is clear throughout man's time and course;
In every step with no remorse,
We push toward our End and Source.

THE MYSTERY

The mystery is
Knowing that as we sit here now,
We're already dead,
Just as certainly
As we're not yet born;
And that every dream
Is a whispered scream
Of hope;
And every breath
Is a bit of death.
We grope
And gasp and rail
Against the tightening grip of
The rope
Around the neck of
Our Eternal Spirit.

THIS IS MY LIFE

My life is like a grade B movie,
Showing on small screens everywhere,
Which is really rather groovy.
Not yet rated by the motion picture industry;
There's too much violence and nudity
In my life.

My life is a revolving smorgasbord
Of anti-depressants and sleeping pills;
And other recreational drugs and diversions
Contributing to society's ills.
And, certainly, I agree this may not be ideal,
Standard behavior; but it's what I feel.

Sometimes I lay on the bed
And curse my own gluttony and sloth.
Maybe someday I'll become
A self-motivated man of the cloth.
The world is changing, and apparently, so am I;
You may not approve, but you cannot deny
That this is my life.
Yes, that's what it is –
It's not hers or his –
This is my life.

INTO THE MOUTH

Oceans teem with life
And we do our best to kill it;
Cities scream with strife
And we cannot seem to still it.
All the things we want and wish
Are as hard to grasp as a flopping fish.
And whether netted or stuck with hook,
We cannot help but steal a look
Into the mouth and dead-eye stare,
Into the vast, unknown despair
That comes with every gasp for air.

NEVER GIVE UP

You did a zig when you needed a zag;
Your centrifugal force had too much drag.
You spilled your milk and cried about it;
Heard the truth but chose to doubt it.
You counted your chickens before they hatched;
Left the surface barely scratched.
You put your head on the chopping block;
Your ship came in and sunk like a rock.
You threw out the baby with the bath water;
Traded the son for a prodigal daughter.
Got kicked in the teeth, punched in the gut,
And all four wheels were stuck in a rut.
You shouted "fire" in a crowded room;
You gave right in to the gloom and doom.
Your number came up, the bottom dropped;
Your market crashed and your engine stopped.
You sold too low and bought too high;
You were gullible and swallowed the lie.
You bit the dust and chewed the fat;
You became the canary-swallowing cat.
You had holes in your socks and two left feet;
A head-on collision on a one-way street.
You sold your thoughts for less than a penny;
Said Yes to drugs and one drink too many.
You've fallen down that slippery slope,
And found a noose at the end of your rope.
You've licked your wounds, down on your luck;
Slept in the back of a pickup truck.
You played the martyr, fell on your sword;
Gave your all for too little reward.
You held your cards when you should have folded,

Italicized when you should have bolded.
You're king of the faux pas, undisputed;
Your audio is fully muted.
Your vines are flush with sour grapes;
Your superheroes lost their capes.
You missed your bus, missed your train;
Left your cake out in the rain.
You fell like Timmy down the well,
And drove the coffin's final nail.
Got caught with your hand in the cookie jar,
Ran your mouth and pushed too far.
You went all-in and saw the flop;
Started crying and could not stop.
Jumped in the fire from the frying pan;
Bought the farm and kicked the can.
Cooked the goose and the golden egg;
Wanted the breast but got the leg.
Lost your way and found some trouble;
Got bad news and burst your bubble.
And to your enemy's great delight,
You painted yourself in a corner tight.
You wasted time and blew your chance;
Lost your way in the great expanse.
You've made mistakes, too many to count;
You've fallen off your trusty mount.
And now the skeletons in your closet
Are pushing on your heart to pause it.
But your enemy is irrelevant,
Whether it's a snake or elephant;
The battle's always won *inside*
With courage, faith, hope and pride.
And though the odds may seem too great,
Never give up or hesitate.

If the hounds of hell are at the gate;
Don't give up or vacillate.
The cusp of crisis will always be
The perch of possibility.
Never give up or in to fear;
Stand for the truth and speak it clear.
And if they run you through with sword,
Roar out with one final chord;
And let this echo in their ear:
You did not bow and you did not fear.
With smiling sneer and bloody spit,
Remind them that you did not quit!
Never give up.
Never give up.
Never give up.

Brunk

ONLY THE BOLD

Only the bold get the most out of life,
Who stretch and reach and strive.
They never give in, never give up,
And they never get buried alive.

For who ever heard of conservative men
Taking a ship to the sky?
Only the bold who want more out of life –
Only the bold would try!

The timid man is afraid of the risk
In reaching for something new.
He seems content to stand back and watch –
Something the bold won't do.

It's a word of wisdom I give free of charge,
Though, really, there's not much to it:
Life is now offered for all to partake,
But only the bold will do it.

MY DOOR

Was that my door?
Is someone there?
Friend or foe, love or hate,
Or something more inanimate?
Could be the wind has blown my door;
Should I get up and close it once more?
Three times already I've closed it for
It's having come open.
How could it be my door
Opens again like before?
Who would be so unrelenting
Pushing ever at my door?
What could they want?
I have nothing to give them,
And nothing to take.

END OF RELATIONSHIP

I felt the stare of thunderclouds
That hovered overhead,
As if to dare the earth to move
Or shake its weary head.

It seemed to me as if the sun
Had finally turned his back
Upon a world that took his warmth
But never offered back.

I heard the wail of multitudes
Who lunged toward the sun,
As if to grasp him by his tail
And keep him under thumb.

Then with a wink, the sun turned round
And blew a playful kiss,
With puckered lips toward the earth
And burned it to a crisp.

REFLECTING UPON SODA POP

Soda pop will lose its fizz
And sparkle when exposed
To air and to the elements.
So, too, a lifetime goes
That bears no hint of poetry
Nor takes the form of prose.

Soda pop is bubbly cold
But when you stop and think,
It can't compare with living life
Nor quench a playful wink.
Life is far more satisfying
And much more fun to drink.

INSIDE MY HEAD

I carry a full-blown universe
Around inside my head,
That no one else can ever see;

An entire civilization
On one proverbial thread,
All descended straight from me;

With every neural star and planet
Composed of joy and dread,
And forever forced to orbit me;
That is, until I cease to be.

And when the Reaper comes to end
The world inside my head;
All of it will cease to be,
Every dream and memory,
Unique to me exclusively,
Erased forever instantly.
And no one else will ever see
The world that lived inside my head.

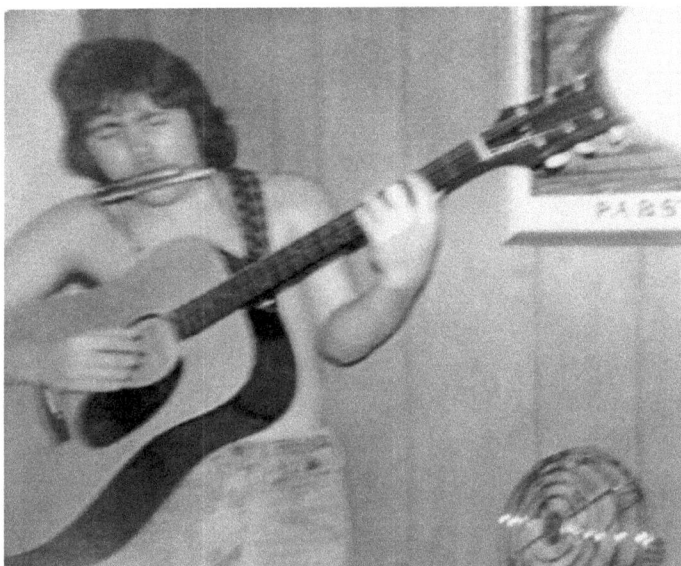

Ron Brunk in 1975 at age 17

Ron Brunk in 2014 at age 55

Ron Brunk Poems
In Chronological Order
(Including exact date of composition if known.)

1976 *(Ron at age 17)*

The Missing Star (2/9/76)
Wind and Rain (3/21/76)
Simply So (3/22/76)
Important Matters (3/23/76)
My Door (3/24/76)
The Ballad of Ted Mills (3/26/76)
The Corpse and the Flea (4/1/76)
Relax (4/8/76)
Opportunistic Poet (4/12/76)
The Noise (4/12/76)
Two Ships Not Passing (4/13/76)
Forfeit (4/14/76)
That Day (4/15/76)
This Peace, I Think (4/24/76)
A Change of Mind

1978 *(age 20)*

Reflecting Upon Soda Pop (12/12/78)
Step Inside (12/12/78)

1982 *(age 23-24)*

The Cycle (2/27/82)
We Must Participate (4/3/82)
Counting Rings (4/15/82)
Crow's Feat (4/15/82)

Nightfall (4/24/82)
Man and Plow (4/29/82)
A Matter of Hemispheres (5/4/82)
The Choice Was Ours (5/5/82)
A Man's Prerogative (5/5/82)
A Summer Rain (5/26/82)
A Grave Visit (5/31/82)
Constellation Lesson (6/25/82)
The Six-Year Silence

1986 *(age 28)*

A Poet's Rights (4/30/86)
Sorrows of the Lawn (4/30/86)
Self-Pity (4/30/86)
The Sure Thing (5/10/86)
Below the Surface (5/10/86)
The Things We Fear (5/13/86)
Only the Bold (5/13/86)
It Seems We're at Our Best When
    We Complain (5/19/86)
Martians (5/21/86)
End of Relationship (5/21/86)
Across the Ages (5/26/86)
A Piece of Nothing

1990 *(age 32)*

Snow Vigil
Love

1992 *(age 34)*

The Driving Force (7/17/92)

1994 *(age 35-36)*

Of Verbs and Tense (4/17/94)
Love and Harsh Reality
Bedtime Prayer
The Wall

1996 *(age38)*

Planet You (12/20/96)

1999 *(age 41)*

The Moon (6/25/99)
The Mystery of It All (6/25/99)
Magic Words (11/26/99)
Coffeehouse Closing
This Is My Life
Shoes
Roscoe

2000 *(age 41-42)*

Idiots (1/12/00)
In the Aftermath of Western Civilization (11/11/00)
Diamonds

2001 *(age 43)*

Grand Design (7/2/01)

2003 *(age 45)*

And She (6/5/03)

2004 *(age 46)*

Off Course (12/28/04)

2006 *(age48)*

Let Go
The Power of Dreams

2011 *(age 53)*

If Our Love Was Eggs (7/11/11)

2013 *(age 55)*

Blaming the Sunshine (11/14/13)
Comfortable (11/16/13)
Bird (12/8/13)
Invention (12/8/13)
Convention (12/8/13)
Catatonic (12/8/13)
Possibilities (12/12/13)

2014 *(age 55)*

Breaking Rank (3/27/14)
Into the Mouth (3/29/14)
The Big Gong (3/31/14)
The Mystery (3/31/14)
Inside My Head (4/3/14)
Never Give Up (4/7/14)
Aging Gracefully Is a Dying Art (4/9/14)

www.ingramcontent.com/pod-product-compliance
Lightning Source LLC
Chambersburg PA
CBHW072357090426
42741CB00012B/3066